Life as we know it

(All truths and no lie)

Erica Pinto

BookLeaf Publishing

India | USA | UK

Presentation by *BookLeaf Publishing*

Web: www.bookleafpub.com

E-mail: info@bookleafpub.com

ISBN: 9789363315990

First edition 2024

*These poems are dedicated to individuals
who feel they are alone in this world.*

Remember,

We are there with you!!

You aren't the only one.

*So, in good times or in bad times, stay
strong, my Friend.*

You will succeed in life.

ACKNOWLEDGEMENT

I would like to express my deepest gratitude to God, my parents and cat, friends and family, and last but not least, my colleagues who inspired me and supported me during this journey.

I owe a part of my personality to you, and whether it be good, bad or ugly, I admire, appreciate, and accept it as it helped me become who I am today.

Thank you!

PREFACE

A book about Our Life.
Yes, that's right, I may know a bit about YOUR
LIFE.

Life as we know it, is a collection of poems that
explores the complexities of relationships,
responsibilities, and the search for self.

These poems are a reflection of my own journey, as
I've navigated the bonds that tie us to others, to our
dreams, and to ourselves.

Through these words, I hope to share a piece of
myself and connect with those who have similar
experiences.

As you read through these pages, I invite you to
reflect on your own bonds – the ones that nourish and
uplift you, as well as those that constrain and
challenge you.

May these poems inspire you to embrace your own
strength, to seek freedom and joy, and to cultivate
love and compassion in all your relationships.

A chance connection

Amidst the crowd, their eyes met
Amidst the commotion, their lips curved into a smile
Amidst the silence, two hearts skipped a beat
Amidst everything, two strangers became friends

From there started the sharing of talks
Going for movies and walks
Their conversations though began with a "Hi"
Never during that time they willingly said "Goodbye"

Of course, this phase was for a short amount of time
The importance given to a person keeps on changing
with the priority line
Amidst all this, they know it in their heart
That the person isn't too far away and just a message
apart

They may no longer sit and chat everyday
But they will always be there for each other, no
matter what others may say
For the bond they built was made on trust
Even unkempt for a while, it won't easily rust

They will always have each other's unwavering
support
When one is down the other will find a way to
provide comfort

Together they will overcome any obstacle, be it an earthquake or a flood
'Cause at the end some relations formed are thicker than blood

They say you come and go from this world alone
But no one told you that you have to live on your own
So, cherish those friendships you find during your lifetime
For in your journey, they will help you to learn and grow, rise and shine.

PRESENT

The power of now

Holding on to yesterday you are losing your present
Wondering about the future you are missing out on
your present
Reminiscing about the hurtful past you are stuck in
your present
Merely hoping for a miracle tomorrow you are not
taking any action in your present

Now imagine living in the present, not for the present
or for today, JUST THE PRESENT

Doing what your heart desires without any fear of
another's judgment
How exciting would it be if only one could live in the
moment

Challenging and working on oneself because without
anyone's consent
That is what life was always meant to be
To learn from history, be ready for a mystery but be
present in the moment for oneself

So, go out there and spread your wings
Nothing impossible just do your thing
And if you find your thoughts running between the
past and future
Remember this line, "Life has never been better."

So, raise your head high and stand strong and tall
It's the present that matters the most of all!!

It's okay to be okay

Nurtured in your mother's womb
Along with your siblings, humble and steady you
grew
Yearning to be the family's favorite child
It's alright if that's not you

Absorbed the words of wisdom from many
Along with batchmates you strove to excel in your
studies
Academically strong but not at the top of the ranks
It's alright if that's not you

Adored by many but your heart sought one
That particular heart which sought not you, but
another one
Don't be disheartened
It's alright if that's not you

Did you work with all your might
You gave it your everything, did all that was right
But the praise was given to another one
It's alright if that's not you

It's alright if you aren't the favorite of all
There is someone out there who values you
It's alright if you aren't a rank holder
You tried your best, that's what matters
It's alright to not aim for the stars and lay low

Don't pressurize yourself, at times just go with the flow
It's alright if you aren't loved by all
You are definitely loved by someone who cares for you
It's alright if you aren't special for everybody
You are meant to be special for yourself

It's alright to be YOU, with all your quirks and charms,
Just being yourself will never cause you any harm
It's alright to be YOU, with all your strength and fears
You're unique and that is what helps you shine through the years.

Who am I?

Cause I am falling
But I have to keep crawling
Because no one wants to see me stop

Cause I am breaking
But I have to keep faking
So that everyone just thinks I'm enough

And I have to force that smile
Though it takes a while
To heal from the hurt

And I have to keep moving on
Cause life goes on
Although I want to burst...

So,
I leave behind all the past that made me, ME

And I don't want to care what others will say about
ME
To take a pause
To rest for a while
To unlearn and learn
Maybe even walk for a mile
To meet new people
To gain more insight
To leave the exterior and read what is inside
To live, laugh, love and die
To do things my way and not answer the millions
why

This is who I am and will be
A brand new and amazing ME
Not afraid of hurt
Not afraid of love
Not afraid to fly like a pure white dove
Not afraid to stand against all the odds
Not afraid to see the sky, although it's filled with
gloomy clouds

This is who I am and will be
Embracing all the chaos within me
Blooming like a flower in the ground
'Cause a part within me which was lost is now found
Flowing like the abundant river source
Moving ahead with an unwavering force

This is who I am and will be,
A strong-willed and hope-filled new me
This is me.

Wish

I wish upon that star so bright
To give you the strength, will and might to fight
I wish upon the sea so deep
That you fall asleep without the urge to weep

I wish upon the forest so dense
That your journey to self-discovery should soon
commence
I wish upon the sun in the day
To cast away the darkness in your life with thy
shining ray

I wish upon that full moon night
To make your worries fade away, make your heart as
a feather light
I wish upon the ground below
To keep you forever humble, no matter how old you
grow

I wish upon the morning dew
To find true friends, don't mind if they are only a few
I wish upon the sky so vast
To give you courage till the very last

I wish upon the innocence of a child
To never let your feelings make you go insane and
wild
I wish upon the mountains up high
That if you stumble from there, you'll not fall but fly

I wish upon the blooming flower
To keep giving you hope, happiness and will-power
I wish upon the seasons in rotation
To help you find your purpose, your own life's
mission

I wish upon the desert so hot
To help you count the blessing you got
I wish upon everything, everything good for you
That you understand your worth, your precious value

Don't let anyone tell you otherwise
IT'S YOUR LIFE—live it with purpose and pride!!

Bonded

Talk about the time
Where you were forced to be present
You had to fake a smile though your heart had been
broken for a while
You didn't want to but had to be around people
As you were bonded with them by blood

Talk about the time
Where you didn't want to go to the mall
As you had to be around people who unknowingly
made you feel small
You didn't want to mingle and wanted to spend that
moment being single
But you had to go as you were bonded under pressure

Talk about the time
Where you didn't want to work for another's dream
Where you had to crush your voice and accept things
as they are
Where you wanted to quit but there would be
repercussions
Hence you stayed
You stayed as you were bonded by finances

Talk about the time
Where you had to sacrifice your personal dreams
To make another collective dream come true
You did it, as you were bonded by a sense of
responsibility

Out of all of them, now talk about the time you did
something for yourself
You were present to feel tall and strong,
You valued your opinion, and strove to achieve your
dream
Although there were hardships, you were still able to
accomplish all of that happily as you were bonded
Bonded by love
Love for oneself!

Death embraced the one I love

My mind is so restless,
Giving me sleepless nights
My heart is aching,
Breaking from inside
My head keeps spinning round and round today..
And it feels like this has been happening every single
day
I gotta stop this storm before it consumes me
I have to forget and move on, leave the past behind
me
So, I gotta go...with the wind near the sea
To let out the voice crushed inside of me
I gotta go...gotta keep moving on
I gotta go...across the gate...across in my lawn
I need to see the light with my eyes to believe it

Only then will I have truly moved on

I know it's no one's fault that you left me
But the concept of that just seems too unfair for me
"Smile for me" were the last words said to me by
you...
But how can I, when you took the reason I smiled,
along with you?
This isn't done, I gotta stop this storm before it
consumes me
I have to forget and move on, leave the hurt filled
memories behind me
So, I gotta go...go away from this town
Before the unpleasant memories give me another
meltdown
I gotta go...gotta keep moving on
With the hope that in our next life, we will meet
again once we are reborn
Till then, I will cherish the memories we spent
together
Hopefully one fine day, I will truly start feeling better
I will be able to see the light beaming from the
horizon
Then you will know, cause my smile will let you, that
from the hurt I have truly moved on...
Our hopes, our dreams, our purpose are all with me
Fulfilling them for us, is my new destiny
So, I gotta go...gotta keep moving on
I will keep living for you, until we meet again...

Rise above the troubles

Do the troubles weigh you down
Submerging you into a corner out there..

Do the troubles weigh on your mind
Like a constant clock ticking out there..

Do you ever wish to break free from the bondages of
life?
Do you ever wish someone was there to hold your
hand while you cry?

Do the troubles keep on growing
Like the leaves of wild creeper

Do the troubles heat your mind up
Like you are in the Sahara desert

Do you ever wish to break free from all the troubles
you face
Do you ever wish someone was there to help you get
through the difficult phase?

So I tell you now, that the troubles aren't all yours to
bear
There are certain unavoidable circumstances and
situations out there..
So don't fret over the things which are out of your
control

Don't get stuck in self-doubt, you have to move away
from that loophole..

There are no right and wrong choices
You have to make yours right..
If you can't avoid a situation
Face it with all of your might..

Don't weigh yourself down with the troubles that
don't seem to end,
Cherish every moment in life, and that will help you
to a great extent..
The troubles will always be around,
But that doesn't mean you go hiding underground..
Rise above your troubles and find your inner peace,
And remember, happiness is always within release!!

Melody of life

Waking up one day, feeling super pumped up,
Going to bed the same day, with your energy real low
Wanting to do things real fast so that you can rush
out,
To ending up feeling tired and exhausted, just want to
take things slow

Is this normal? Is this natural?
Is there anyone out there who finds this relatable?
Your life at a moment feels like a rollercoaster ride
Feel like you're struggling to balance your surfboard
on a huge tide..
One second you are up, next minute you are down
In a jiffy your happiness can turn into a frown..

But that's what life is about,
Don't beat yourself in self-doubt..
You rise or that's not the end, it's just a phase,
You may hit a few blocks before you navigate
yourself out of the maze..
The moment you hit rock bottom, remember that
doesn't stay long enough,
Blink and see you've reached the top and your mind
has become tough..

Is this a good thing? Or is it bad?
Don't remain upset with the time and get mad..
Find your rhythm and find your own way,

Stay on the track and you may not sway..
And even if you get lost for a while,
Your well wishers will be waiting for you and when
you arrive, they will greet you with a smile..

Play the tune meant for you,
Only you have the authority to change it, only you
can see the end view..
In the journey of life, find your voice,
Learn to trust your gut, your inner choice..
So, keep moving on and don't give up the pace,
Find your own rhythm in life's race!!

Was that love?

Shy since birth, I crawled my way into the youthful world
Concentrating on good grades, steering away from pleasures unknown to me
Caught my glimpse was a perfect face that made my heart flutter like never before
It made me wonder, is this love?

That perfect face seemed to master the art of chivalry
Good to all, but a bit more special to me (or that's what I felt)
Deep down in my mind I knew you were already taken
But my heart yearning for compassion couldn't see otherwise and made me wonder
Is this really love?

Truth be told, at times our weary mind turns a blind
eye
For we are unable to spot the red concealed within
the green
The impulse to be loved comes with a force so strong
and tight
That our heart seems to ignore the difference between
what's wrong and right
We seem to wonder if we are really in love?

When the mind and heart aren't on the same page
And you find it difficult to place an anchor to stop the
ship from going with the waves
You need a little help from an angel above
But since God couldn't send angels in their true form,
true friends came along
Those friends who help you realize what is love

Uncovered then was the truth of all
I am special for some, don't need to be for all
Of course, the pain of not being special for that
perfect face lingered for sometime
But little did I know it helped me gain the experience
of a lifetime
Love can be shared but can't be attached to another
being

Remembering that time makes me giggle a bit
Cause no one is perfect we all are misfits
So, if you feel someone is a complete ten
Let me tell you, your mind is tired and playing a trick

Only your true friends will realize it and help you
heal and fix

Speaking from experience let me tell you this
Happiness should come from self rather than others
Cause no one, I repeat, no one should love you more
than you should love yourself
Keep yourself as your first priority
And just take a step back to witness how beautiful
life can and will be.

The Phoenix Rises

There comes a point in everyone's life
Where nothing seems to work out no matter how hard
you strive
The world may seem to be working against your
favor at the moment
You might want to take a step back, lay low, remain
dormant
Everything around you seems like it's moving too fast
or either you are in slow-mo
You start feeling helpless and your emotions and
energy run low
Each breath, a struggle and living feels like an
eternity
All the shadows of self-doubt in your heart and mind,
driving you to insanity

Let me tell you today that this moment will surely
fade
Like the gray sky that eventually yields to radiant
shade
Take your time to heal and move away from the
traumatizing past
Only moments of pure delight are meant forever to
last
So let go of the baggage you carry
There is no need to rush and be in a hurry
Now rise from the ashes my Phoenix, spread your
wings and fly

You may have touched rock bottom, but now you
only have one way to go and that's up high
So unlock the cage, spread your wings
You will realize how beautiful life is once you start
appreciating the little things
Move ahead with a gratitude-filled heart, and you
will surely not need to fake that smile
True happiness will come to you, for special people
at times it takes a while
Be like the bird you were meant to be
Moving freely, spreading joy and glee, wild and
carefree.

Beyond the crowd

Millions of people, you will come across your
lifetime,
Not all will be perfect, but some will turn out just
fine..
Some may make you stronger, whereas others may
make you softer,
Here your mind is wondering, who among them are
meant to remain a bit longer...

'Cause, thousands of folks you meet every single
year,
Some meant to stay near whereas others kind of with
the crowd tend to disappear..
The ones who will know you in numbers will be quiet
a few
As the rest of them won't seem interested to know the
real you...

Hundreds of sounds are heard for almost sixteen
hours every single day,

Telling you what to do, how to behave, what to say..
But none of them, tell you what you really want to
hear,
Something which will help you forget your fears...

They will tell you to stay stable, so that you will be
able to go somewhere,
Little do they know that your dream is to jump and
fly away...
There's no more hiding, no more staying behind
closed doors,
You need to move out to explore the horizon, cause
you want so much more...

So listen close, listen hard, to the voice within your
head,
All your fears, all your troubles you will need them to
shed..
Close your eyes and look down deep, cause the
answer is within you,
Trust me you don't need to fake it, just have patience
and stay true...

Out of the Hundreds of people you know,
There will be some with whom your relation will
grow..
For better or for worse,
They will make an impact on you, might even change
your universe...

And if by chance, darkness falls and you're left
alone,

Don't sit there to cry and mourn..
Stand up on your feet to see others around who are
true,
The ones who care and love you for being you...

Never in your life will you be entirely on your own,
You have millions of memories with you, always
engraved within your soul...
So cherish them with all your heart,
And hold them close like embers that never depart...

Beyond the crowds, within the depths of your soul,
A world of wonder awaits, where you are whole...
See yourself in bits and parts, in every way..
Embrace your truth, go out there to seize your day..
Remember no one knows you better than you,
Trust yourself and your power will breakthrough!!

Strength in Resilience

Life in itself isn't super simple,
I know you tried hard to fake a smile and show that
dimple..
At times you might feel that the troubles weigh you
down,
And you may want to escape from the people near
you in that town..
The hurt and pain may be the only things you feel
currently,
But this time too shall pass, eventually..
It might seem right, however running from a problem
isn't always a healthy solution,
You may need to try different ways and means to
come to a resolution..
Just remember, you're stronger than you seem and
you know it,
Look back, see those other problems, didn't you fix
it..
You deserve it, so for a while take a break,
Life will always offer you another retake..

Ask for help, if you think something is too tough,
But on yourself don't be so rough..
Look at the mirror and repeat this every day,
I will live for myself no matter what others may say!
In the future, trust me everything will be fine,
You're going to rise, you're going to soar, like a star,
you're going to shine..
So, hang in there my friend, hang in there for a while,
Make your mind and heart strong, not weak and
fragile..
Nothing in life needs to remain constant,
So, learn to love, live, and enjoy the happy moments..
Good things take time, so please have patience and
wait,
Trust in yourself, and have a bit of hope and faith..
When times are difficult, lean on those joyful
memories,
And see how a mystical force will indirectly push
you ahead in your life journeys!!

Embracing your true self

They say, "Words cut sharper than a sword,"
Whatever you say and hear is absorbed by the heart
and kept in your mind's record..
The heart, so naive, unknowingly believes those
words to be true,
Slowly with time you start forgetting who used to be
the real you..

Thousands of cabinets placed within your mind,
Holding personality bits of people you find..
Day in day out you open those drawers,
To use one of those findings and get done with your
chores..

The fear of being called out, compels you to wake up
at night,
In this race of life, you are tired of the constant fight..

The fight to prove your worth to others puts you in
stress,
Year over year, you're struggling to cope up with your
neighbours' success..

But is that truly what you wanted to be?
Wasn't your dream in childhood to go out and run,
jump and play and be free..
Chasing the dreams of others will get you nowhere,
Cause that wasn't yours to begin with, to be really
fair..

Stop moving along with the herd,
You are an individual, not an animal or bird..
I know it seems difficult with the responsibilities you
have to fulfill,
But look down deep in your heart, wouldn't it feel
good to pursue a hobby with your own free will?

Out of twenty-four hours in a day, try to take one to
do the thing you love,
Slowly you will see the way your emotions will turn
better and eventually lift you above..
Among all those drawers in your brain,
Try to seek the one which is truly you (this may take
a bit of time and pain)..

Seek the moments in which you're the happiest,
The activities you did at that time are the ones which
you do the best..
Do those a bit more as and when you get the time,

And your life will slowly and steadily get back in
line..

Trust your instinct! It matters more than others'
acknowledgement,
Do what you like without the fear of people's
judgment..
In this way, you will learn new aspects about
yourself, what gives you a thrill, and what makes you
ill,
Embrace all those parts of you, as it's your life, so
live it as you will!!

Shattered but Unbroken

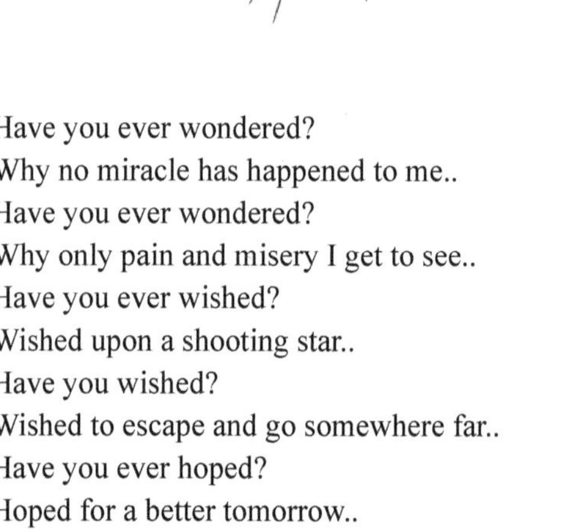

Have you ever wondered?
Why no miracle has happened to me..
Have you ever wondered?
Why only pain and misery I get to see..
Have you ever wished?
Wished upon a shooting star..
Have you wished?
Wished to escape and go somewhere far..
Have you ever hoped?
Hoped for a better tomorrow..
Have you ever hoped?
Hoped to be free from all the hurt and sorrow..
Have you ever thought?
Will I be able to overcome this despair..
Have you ever thought?
Am I so broken, beyond the scope of repair..

So, my friend, I will tell you now...
Read loud and clear now..

Miracles...they come in various sizes, big and small,
They are meant for you and for all..
Don't you realize, when you wake up each and every
day,
That itself is a miracle in its way..
And when you look around the ecosystem,
Isn't that a miracle in God's Kingdom..

Although you may feel like you're broken,
Have words and emotions unspoken...
Like the pieces of colored tiles that have been
shattered,
Your feelings and thoughts at the moment are
scattered...

All you need is hope and patience, my friend,
Your life will get better or else that ain't the end..
And then one day, maybe with a bit of help or even
by yourself,
You will gather the broken bits and pieces and create
a pattern within your mind's shelf...

It will contain every bit of you, that is whole and
true...
It doesn't need to be perfect, but it needs to be and
will be YOU!!

Fight your fears

Afraid of reptiles crawling near your skin,
Well, that's one thing similar among all of our kin..
Worried about the eyes glaring at you,
Wondering if they are currently judging the things
you do..
Too scared to speak the words out aloud,
Pondering if you will suddenly become the focus of
the crowd..
Fearing the unknown,
You are leaving the seeds unsown..

Why? Why? Why are you hiding in your room, up all
curled?
Why? Why? Why are you letting anxiety take control
of your world?

Hold on to the light and move away from the
darkness
Remember one thing my friend you are extremely
precious

There is nothing that is impossible...
You don't need to feel that you're invisible
And it's perfectly normal and fine for you to feel
emotional
No matter what anyone tells you, you've got to
believe you are sensible

It's alright if getting through your fears doesn't seem
too simple
But remember this, it isn't something that is incurable

So please, please don't be so rigid in giving up on life
in all,
Try a new approach and embrace the concept of
being flexible..
Eventually things will turn out right and you will be
indispensable..

And then you'll show them all, what your dear ones
knew from the start,
That YOU ARE INCREDIBLE, a shining work of
art!

Unapologetically Me!

I'm skeptical
Sometimes a little bit irrational
I have no intention to hurt your feelings
But that somehow happens when we have an
unplanned meeting

I'm delusional
Sometimes a little bit impractical
I have no intention to disagree with you
But that somehow happens when I try to be true

You may think, I might be childish,
And that I lack a sense of maturity
But trust me when I say to you now
That I know my duty and responsibility

I'm emotional
Sometimes a little bit unsociable
But at times I just want to spend time alone
And that's why I don't answer my damn cellphone

I'm approachable
Generally, people think I'm a bit motivational
But I just speak from my personal experience
Not complaining but I have gone through a fair share
of grievance

Some may think, I might be depressed
But don't worry, I'm only a bit stressed
Things will get better once I take rest
'Cause deep down in my heart I know I'm abundantly
blessed
And I know I don't need to worry
'Cause I've got my close friends and my family
And I have someone who cares deeply for me
So I know even if the world doesn't accept me
I don't need to try to convince everybody
Since I'm perfect in just being Me
And that's all that matters at all,
Embracing my individuality and standing strong and
tall!!

The Tides of Change

The look that drove me crazy at one time, no longer does the same..
The voice that swept me off my feet, no longer sounds the same..
The person who was with me 24/7, no longer is the same...
Cause people, yes people, THEY CHANGE..

The people who used to care at one time, no longer keep in touch..
The people who were around me at the time, no longer are the same..
The salary figure kept in mind, that number has increased ten times..
Cause priorities, yes priorities, THEY CHANGE..

The things that were important at one time, no longer are the same..
The places that I visited every year no longer look the same..
The dialogue that hit me hard at sometime, no longer makes me feel uneasy..
Cause emotions, yes emotions, THEY CHANGE..

The time that felt difficult in the past, feels like a piece of cake now..
The percentages that mattered long ago, aren't so relevant right now..

The palace that the neighbours owned, seems entirely small now..
Cause Life, yes Life, IT CHANGES..

And is it so bad that Life changes?
I feel not..
And is it so bad that people move on?
I feel not..
Cause without change, without change, we would be stuck on something for a while,
Keeping unrealistic expectations, leading to our downfall sometime..

And without change, without change, we wouldn't be able to up our game in evolution..
To better ourselves and find problems, solutions..
Therefore change, therefore change, is essential and that is what makes it so very special!!

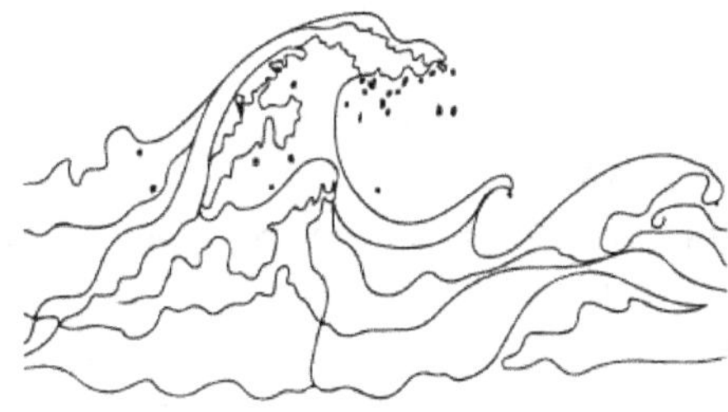

Why me?

The pain you felt when your heart broke for the
zillionth time,
Asking yourself the question out there, why couldn't
they be mine?
You beat yourself into overthinking
Wondering why did you ever catch feelings
And out came the question in your mind..
Why me? Why only me? Why does it hurt so bad?

The pain you felt when the results betrayed the
preparation you did,
Unknowingly those around you compared you with
the next-door kid,
You beat yourself to prove your worth
And in that moment you didn't feel like remaining on
this planet earth
And out came the question in your mind..
Why me? Why only me? Why do I feel so bad?

The pain you felt when the one you loved left you,
The world seemed so different, everything seemed so
strange and new,
You beat yourself into thinking what else could you
do?
To relive the time spent together and make more
memories too
And out came the question in your mind..
Why me? Why only me? Why does it feel so bad?

Little do you know, there are plenty in this world like
you,
Searching for love, but facing heartbreaks too..
Not knowing how to move on,
Thinking they are all alone..
Running away from other people,
Hesitating to pick up the phone..

They faced the loss,
Are tossed across,
They are devastated..
They are treated like a vermin,
Are broken from within,
They are entirely exhausted..

You're not alone, you're not alone, in the universe
You're not alone, you're not alone, so don't you dare
feel like you're cursed
You're a special one, my dear, don't lose hope, don't
lose sight

You will get through the hard times, just keep faith
and fight with your might

Don't ask the question, Why me?
Everything will be fine, just trust me..
It's not you, I promise..
It's the situation that is tough,
Which will make you in the future strong and rough..
It's not you, I promise..
There are better days ahead in the future,
So don't you dare give up with the pressure...
It's not you, I promise..
There are others like you on this earth,
Believe in your instincts and know your worth..
It's not you, I promise..
You are wonderful the way you are,
In the end, you will succeed and go somewhere far!!

Personalities

You might be an extrovert or an introvert,
Love to mix around or may be shy at first..
Decide based on facts and concepts or just go with
your gut,
Maybe a crazy cat person, or love to play with a
mutt...
You may want to party hard, or might be the one to
sleep in low,
Want to reach the heights real fast, or take it calm and
slow..
You can lead the pack or even help around,
Might want to fly in the air or stay close to the
ground..
You may want to steer up the crowd or hide and
escape from it,
Might be too tired to go for a run, or be extremely
fit..
You can be a studious one, or just want to play and
have fun,
Might be extremely wealthy or not have a ton..
You may be a people pleaser or can speak your mind,
One can call you rude or may feel you're too kind..
It might be easy for you to make decisions, or maybe
you like to change along the way..
All of what you do really matters, as much as what
you think and say..
You may want to learn from the past and your history,
or might have a futuristic view of things,

With self-belief the sky can be your limit, so go out
there and spread out your wings..
You can be anything you want to be,
Don't be embarrassed, just embrace your personality..
There is nothing wrong with you, that's just who you
are,
Keep loving yourself for what you are!

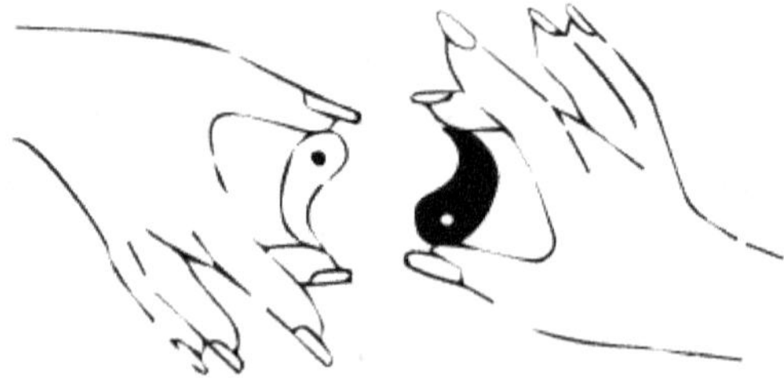

Love through the seasons

Summer brings out sunlight and harshness in some,
But not in the one I speak to daily—my mum
The rays are so strong that it drives me mad
But I'm sheltered by a parasol, held by my dad
Woahoooooh oooooh, that's the people around me..

Spring comes with the flowers blooming on the earth
Troubled by the stress, I question my self-worth
And there comes those voices, "We need to have a
word"
From friends who care too much and don't want me
to have thoughts which are absurd
Woahoooooh oooooh, that's the people around me..

While the leaves disown the trees during Autumn
There are few thoughts that hit my brain, which are
so random
Wondering if I can do anything to change the existing
unfair system

The people near me tell me it's possible with
everyone's support and wisdom
Woahoooooh oooooh, that's the people around me..

The rain brings out a sweetness in the air,
It's the season where we notice who really does care
'Cause those days when you will leave your umbrella
at home
There will be someone sheltering you with the one
they own
Woahoooooh oooooh, that's the people around me..

Winter comes along the way, surrounding the area
with its cold breeze
There are some people who connect with others with
such ease
They care for their near and dear ones, and help them
do what's good for them as they please
They're perfect for each other and go together like
mac and cheese
Woahoooooh oooooh, that's the people around me..

The one's with me through all the seasons,
Who knows if I am upset along with the reasons
Who stick with me through thick and thin,
Who know me personally from within
Those are the SPECIAL ones
The PRECIOUS ones
The ever FORGIVING ones
Those are the people around me.

Crossroads

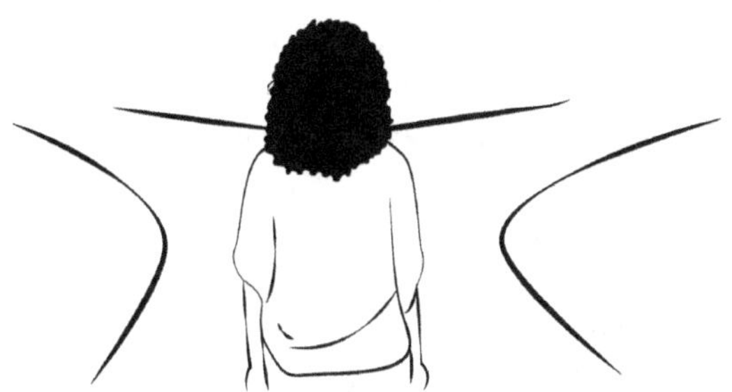

Standing at the crossroads, waiting to decide
Pondering on situations, seeking the answer from inside..
Where will this road take me?
Will it make me or break me?
How will I cope if I fail?
Is my thought new or is it stale?

Standing at the crossroads, waiting for a guide to come my way,
Time goes by and it's moving fast, and I can no longer differentiate between night and day..
What's there in my future?
I'm crushed by that pressure
What will I do if I fall to the ground?
How will I come out if I'm stuck under a mound?

Standing at the crossroads, wondering how life will unfold,

Will life be kind and warm to me or will I be stuck in
the cold
All these thoughts and words are in my head
Anxiety and worries are being well-fed..
What will I do? where will I go if all is lost,
The decisions I make have an impact on cost..

There came a known one up front,
Spoke to me, wordings real blunt
Won't keep it a secret from you
Cause you deserve to succeed in all
Stop standing there and beating yourself up the wall...
"There are no right choices in life, you make your
choices right"
Give it a fight, don't lose sight
Give it your all, don't worry about the fall..
You may think you are weak and small
But you are not, trust me my friend,
You will give it your best and move on till the very
end..

Crossroads will be plenty, making you to choose
Don't panic, there is no right or wrong in them,
you've got nothing to lose
So go forth, and choose with courage in your heart,
Believe in yourself and you'll find your way from the
start..
Though the choices you make, will change your life,
I'm sure it will be for the best,
Cause my friend you are, and will always, be blessed!

A life of Blessings

Blessed, 'cause I have a roof above my head,
Blessed, 'cause I have teeth to savor the bread...
When times get tough and I feel drained out low,
I'm still blessed, 'cause I get to go to sleep on a bed..

Blessed, for the family I know,
Blessed, how they've helped me to grow..
They rejoice in my happiness and are with me even
when I'm sad,
They're a part of my life, for that I'm super glad..

Blessed, for the work that I do,
Blessed, 'cause it has helped me broaden my view..
Pleased with the colleagues whom I work with,
At times, workplace politics just feels like a myth..

Blessed, for the friends in my life,
Blessed, 'cause they help me survive..
They know when I'm faking and not feeling fine,
Blessed 'cause they better me, and help to shine..

Blessed, for being a part of nature,
Blessed, 'cause I get to see every plant and every
creature..
They embrace change and make the world seem
perfectly beautiful,
They teach us values of giving and being so ever
merciful..

I'm just blessed for all the things, be it big or small,
I know I'm blessed cause I have it all..

In a world filled with times, where we only see what
other people own,
It's time we count the blessings we have and see what
we own..
It may seem different but it will be a part of you,
It will be amazing and to its core it will be true..
You are blessed, and are being blessed in every way,
Remember that and you will shine my friend, shine
every single day!

www.ingramcontent.com/pod-product-compliance
Lightning Source LLC
Chambersburg PA
CBHW061719130726
47996CB00006B/2405